Mel Bay Presents

Medieval & Renaissance
Music for Folk Harp

arranged by Laura Zaerr

Cover photo by Bob Furguson

1 2 3 4 5 6 7 8 9 0

Visit us on the Web at www.melbay.com — E-mail us at email@melbay.com

Contents

Medieval Songs

Renaissance Dances

Historical Notes on the Music

Eleventh century France witnessed the rise of musicians of all sorts. The jongleurs (jugglers) traveled as itinerant musicians from town to town playing traditional folk music for entertainment in the streets. The Troubadours and Trouvères, on the other hand, boasted a noble birth, and generally had plenty of time to kill to write love songs and poetry expressive of a long courtly tradition of chivalry. They enjoyed the golden patronage of kings and princes, not the paltry centimes of the peasantry.

The Trouvères (trouver = to find) predominated in the north of France, distinguished by their language, langed'oil, French. Their counterparts in southern France, the Troubadours (trobar=to find) spoke lange d'oc, Provençal. These southerners flourished under the patronage of a vibrant Mediterranean aristocracy, a culture which faced economic devastation after the Albigensian crusade (1209-1229) when the ravaging armies of Simon de Montfort swept through Provence. These poets and musicians suddenly found themselves destitute, dispersing to Spain and Italy.

Their cousins to the north fared somewhat better. In the 12th C. Trouvère songs were highly influenced by those of the troubadours. In 1137 Eleanor of Aquitaine, grand-daughter of Guillaume de Poitiers, moved to Paris as the queen of King Louis VII. Of course she brought with her a cadre of poets and musicians whose music reminded her of her homeland in southern France. Soon the Trouvères in northern France had developed their own characteristic traits, including a somewhat epic and heroic quality. The long-lived culture of the Trouvères allowed a vast amount of material to be documented, about 1,400 melodies and 4,000 poems, which were often mixed and matched. In fact one could say the roots of western music can be traced to this body of work.

Trouvère music is monophonic, having a single clear melody line. No one knows for sure how these songs were accompanied, but probably veille (early fiddle), lute and harp would feature prominently. The text of these strophic songs falls into several genres which include *canso*, a courtly love-song; *dansa*, based on a dance form; *pastorela*, an amorous encounter between a knight and a shepherdess as in *Quant voi la feur nouvele*; and *planh*, a lament. The formes fixes (*rondeau, virelai* and *ballade*) appear toward the end of the period. The *virelai* has a musical structure ABBAA, with the first and last sections having the same lyrics, as is *Douce dame jolie* and *Ay mi! Dame de valolur*.

Minnesangen (songs of courtly love) come into popularity in Germany roughly between 1200 to 1300. *Minne* is the High Middle German word for love. The marriage of Frederick Barbarossa with Beatrix of Burgundy in 1156 speaks of the cultural interchange between Germany and France. Like their French counterparts, the Minnesingers sprung from the noble class.

Freidrich von Hausen (c.1155-1190) was one of the earliest Minnesingers who traveled extensively in France and Provence, bringing back with him the French esthetic of Courtly Love. He was killed in battle while accompanying the emperor Freidrich Barbarossa on the Crusade of 1189. Legend has it that the entire army mourned his death.

By the time of **Neidhart von Reuental** (c.1180-1237/46) German Minnesingers were developing their own distinctive voice free from French influences. Neidhart, like von Hausen, also toured the middle-east on a crusade, but he managed to stay alive. Neidhart's poetry differs from the classic Minnesinger traditions in that he introduces a humorous, often satirical streak, reflecting his own lowly peasant background. He gained and retained so much popularity that his was the only Minnesinger music to be published into the Renaissance. Reuental is most likely a pseudonym, meaning valley of lamentation. Notice how he uses this name in the text of *So Blozen wir den anger*.

Meanwhile, in the fair city of Castile Spain, **King Alfonso X** "el sabio" (the wise) (1221-1284) kept himself busy writing extensively on jurisprudence, and studying science. In his spare time he wrote and collated a huge body of musical texts called Cantigas (songs). Written in Galician Portuguese, the poetry is classified as "Moorish-Andalusian", a fascinating study of East meets West. *420 Cantiagas de Santa Maria* extol the virtues of St. Mary in hymns and in miraculous feats of faith. Bailemos is an example of a *Cantiga d'amigo*, a love song in the same genre.

Giorgio Mainerio (c. 1530-40-1582) lived in Udine, Italy. He often signed his name Mayner, possibly because his father was Scottish. Being attracted to the occult, astrology and necromancy, he was a natural target for the inquisition, which fate he managed to sidestep. Besides writing some semi-hit tunes such as *Ungaresca* and *Scharazula Marazula*, he published mostly sacred music, and a lovely set of dances in 1578 in which these two dances appear.

Giovanni Giacomo Gastoldi (c.1550–c.1622) was born in the small town of Caravaggio, named after the famous painter who was 10 years Gastoldi's junior. The young musician served as the maestro di cappella for the Gonzaga family in Mantua, but eventually moved to Milan. He is known for his light and rhythmically lively balletti, vocal dance music, of which *Speme Amoroso* is a prime example.

Tielman Susato (c.1500-1561) was a Renaissance man in every sense. Much like musicians today his musical career encompassed performing (sackbut or early trombone, recorder and crumhorn), publishing, printing, composing, arranging, diplomacy, and calligraphy. He set up a flourishing publishing business in Antwerp in 1541, and the rest is history. The dances presented here represent a common repertoire in the Franco Flemish high society of the 16th century.

Notes on the Translations and Editing

A special thanks to Linda Marie Zaerr for translations of *Voulez vous que je vous chant, Ay mi! Dame de valour, Quant je voi yver,* and *Bailemos,* as well as editing the other French texts. Also a special thanks to Jeff Parsons for editing the historic notes and the German translations. Thanks also to Noah Brenner for his music editing expertise.

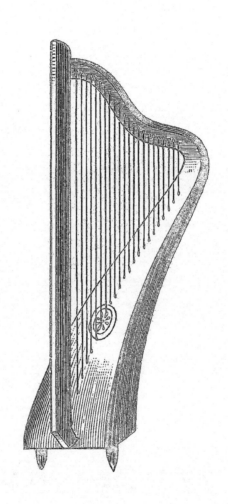

Douce dame jolie

Guillaume de Machaut

Douce dame jolie

lever slide

Douce dame jolie

Guillaume de Machaut (c.1300-1377)

Douce dame jolie,
Pour dieu ne pensés mie
Que nulle ait signorie
Seur moy fors vous seulement.

Qu'adès sans tricherie Chierie
Vous ay et humblement
Tous les jours de ma vie Servie
Sans villain pensement.

Helas! et je mendie
D'esperance et d'aïe;
Dont ma joie est fenie,
Se pité ne vous en prent.

Douce dame jolie…

Mais vo douce maistrie Maistrie
Mon cuer si durement
Qu'elle le contralie et lie
En amour tellement

Qu'il n'a de riens envie
Fors d'estre en vo baillie;
Et se ne li ottrie
Vos cuers nul aligement.

Douce dame jolie...

Et quant ma maladie Garie
Ne sera nullement
Sans vous, douce anemie, Qui lie
Estes de mon tourment,

A jointes mains deprie
Vo cuer, puis qu'il m'oublie,
Que temprement m'ocie,
Car trop langui longuement.

Douce dame jolie...

Sweet, lovely lady
for god's sake do not think
that any has sovereignty
over my heart, but you alone.

For always, without treachery, cherished
Have I you, and humbly
All the days of my life served
Without base thoughts.

Alas, I am left begging
For hope and relief;
For my joy is at its end
Without your compassion.

Sweet, lovely lady....

But your sweet mastery masters
My heart so harshly,
Tormenting it and binding
In unbearable love,

[My heart] desires nothing
but to be in your power.
And still, your own heart
renders it no relief.

Sweet, lovely lady....

And since my malady
Will not be annulled
Without you, Sweet Enemy,
Who takes delight of my torment

With clasped hands I beseech
Your heart, that forgets me,
That it mercifully kill me
For too long have I languished.

Sweet lovely lady…

Li joliz temps d'estey

13th C. France

Li joliz temps d'estey

Li joliz temps d'estey

Li joliz temps d'estey
Trouvére

Li joliz temps d'estey
Que je voi revenir,
Et Amors, qui donney
M'a le douz souvenir
De ma dame que desir,
Mi font joie mener
Et dire amorousement:
Je les sent, dex, je les sent
Les mans d'amer doucement.

Ploins de joliveté
En espir d'amanrir
Ma tres douce grietey
Don't je ne quier garir,
Tant aing si douz mal soffrir
Que ne puis oublier
Que ne die houtement;
Je les sent....

Trop me soi mal garder
Quant premiers l'acointai,
Quant, por li resgarder
Me prist li maus que j'ai.
Douz Dex, se je s'amor ai,
Encor porrai chanter
Et dire envoisiement::
Je les sent....

Nuns hons ne puet durer
Sanz amours, bien le sai.
Por ce vuil endurer
Les gries max que je trai,
Et touz jors, tant con vivrai,
Servirai sanz fauser
Ma dame por cui je chant::
Je les sent....

Sentir les me covient
Les joliz maux dAmer;
Mais l'amors qui me tient
Fera trop a blasmer
Se celi que n'ox nommer
Ne saisist et retient
Si qu'ele die en chantant::
Je les sent....

Summer has returned and with it the desire to love. Remembering the lover is both sweet and full of sorrow. Love is a malady, but wants no cure; desire and pain are inseparably linked with each other. At first sight of the lover the man was already overcome with yearning for her. Since no man can live without love, he intends to endure his suffering patiently until death, and to serve his lady always in unshakeable faith. He hopes that she will eventually listen to him.

Voulez vous

13th C. France

Voulez vous

Trouvére

Voulez vous que je vous chant
Un son d'amors avenant?
    Vilain ne fist mie,
Ainz le fist un chavalier
Souz l'onbre d'un olivier
    Entre les braz s'amie.

Chemisete avoit de lin
Et blanc peliçon hermin
    Et bliaut de soie,
Chauces ot de jaglolai
Et sollers de flors de mai,
    Estroitement chauçade.

Cainturete avoit de fueille
Qui verdist quant li tens mueille;
    D'or ert boutonade.
L'aumosniere estoit d'amour;
Li pendant furent de flor,
    Par amors fu donade.

Si chevauchoit une mule;
D'Argent ert la ferreure,
    La sele ert dorade;
Seur la crope par derrier
Avoit planté trois rosiers
    Por fere li honbrage.

Si s'en vet aval la pree;
Chevalieres l'ont encontree,
    Biau l'ont saluade:
"Bele, dont estes vous nee?"
"De France sui, la loee,
    Du plus haut parage."

"Li rosignous est mon pere
Qui chante seur la remee
    El plus haut boscage;
La seraine, ele est ma mere
Qui chante en la mer salee
    El plus haut rivage.

"Bele, bon fussiez vous nee,
Bien estes enparentee
    Et de haut parage;
Pleust a Dieu nostre pere
Que vous me fussiez donee
    A fame espousade."

Would you like for me to sing a song of love?
It was not composed by a churl, but by a knight,
Under the shade of an olive tree,
between the arms of his love.

She was wearing a linen under tunic
and a white ermine mantle and silk tunic.
She was tightly shod in stockings of iris flowers
and shoes of May flowers.

Her belt was made of leaves
which turned green in moist weather;
it was buttoned with gold.
Her purse was made of love,
with flowers dangling down.
It was given for love.

She rose a mule shod with silver
with a golden saddle.
On it's crupper behind her were planted
three rose bushes to give her shade.

As she rode through the meadow
knights who met her greeted her courteously:
"Lovely one, where were you born?"
"I am from famous France, of the highest lineage.

"The nightingale, who sings
on the highest branch in the grove is my father;
the siren who sings on the highest bank
of the salt sea, is my mother."

"Lovely one, you are well born.
Fine is your parentage, of the highest lineage.
May it please God our father
that you might be given to me as my wife."

Ay mi! Dame de valour

Guillaume de Machaut

Ay mi! Dame de valour

Ay mi! Dame de valour
Guillaume de Machaut

Ay mi! dame de valour
que j'aim et desir,
de vous me vient la dolour
qui me fait languir.

Tre douce creature,
comment puet vo fine doucour
estre vers moy si dure,
quant mon cuer, Mon corps et m'amour

Vous ay donné sans retour
et sans repentir?
Or me tenez en languor
dont je criem morir.

Ay mi! dame de valour…

Et tout par amesure,
gentil dame, pleinne d'onnour,
sui je a desconfiture;
car onque ne quis deshonnour

Vers vous, ains ay sans sejour
fait vo dous plasir
et feray sans mauvais tour
jusques au morir.

Ay mi! dame de valour…

Mais vo douce figure,
vo fine biaute que j'aour
et vo noble faiture
paree de plaisant atour

En plour tiennent nuit et jour,
sans joie sentir,
mon cuer qui bit en tristour,
dont ne puet garir.

Ay mi! dame de valour…

Alas! Noble lady,
whom I love and desire,
from you comes the sadness
which causes me to languish.

Very sweet creature,
how can your refined gentleness
be so hard toward me,
since I have unswervingly given

my heart, my body, and my love,
without regret?
Now you hold me in a languishing state
which I fear may cause me to die.

Alas, noble lady…

It does not accord,
sweet and honorable lady,
that I be so distressed,
for I sought nothing dishonorable

To you but have always with out stinting,
done your sweet pleasure,
and I will do so, without trickery,
until death.

Alas, noble lady…

But your sweet face,
your refined beauty that I love,
and your noble person,
adorned with pleasing embellishment

Keep my heart in tears,
night and day, without feeling any delight,
and thus it lives in sadness
whence it cannot be cured.

Alas noble lady…

Ecco la primavera

Francesco Landini

Ecco la primavera

Ecco la primavera
Francesco Landini (c. 1335-1397)

Ecco la primavera
Che 'l cor fa rallegrare,
temp' è d'annamorare'
e star con lieta cera.

No'vegiam l'aria e 'l tempo
che pur chiam' allegreça.
in questo vago tempo
ogni cosa a vagheça.

L'erbe con gran frescheça
e fior' coprono i prati,
e gli alberi adornati
sono in simil manera.

Ecco la primavera
Che 'l cor fa rallegrare,
temp' è d'annamorare'
e star con lieta cera.

Behold the springtime,
which makes the heart rejoice;
it is the season to fall in love
and to be happy.

We enjoy that air and weather
which itself may be called happiness;
in this lovely season
everything takes on loveliness.

The grass with great freshness
and flowers cover the fields;
and the trees, all decked out,
are wearing the same fashion.

Behold the springtime,
which makes the heart rejoice;
it is the season to fall in love
and to be happy.

Je demande ma bienvenue

Jean Haucourt

Je demande ma bienvenue

Je demande ma bienvenue

Jean Haucourt (c. 1390-1410)

Je demande ma bienvenue:
"Il a longtemp que ne vous vi;
Dites, suit je plus vostre ami;
Avés bien vostre foy tenue?"

La meilleur desoubs la nue
estes se l'avés fait ensi."

Je demande na bienvenue:
"Il a longtemps que ne vous vi."

Je vous ai moult longtemps perdue.
Dont j'ay esté en grant soussi,
mais de tous mes maulx sui gari,
puis qu'en bon point je vous ay veue".

Je demande ma bienvenue:
"Il a longtemp que ne vous vi;
Dites, suit je plus vostre ami;
Avés bien vostre foy tenue?"

I ask my sweet-heart:
"I have not seen you for a long time;
Tell me, am I still your love;
Have you kept faith with me?

You are the most faithful woman
On Earth if you have.

I ask my sweet heart,
"I have not seen you for a long time."

I have been parted from you for a very long time,
which has made me very unhappy.
But I am cured of all my ills,
now that I have found you well.

I ask my sweet-heart:
"I have not seen you for a long time;
Tell me, am I still your love;
Have you kept faith with me?

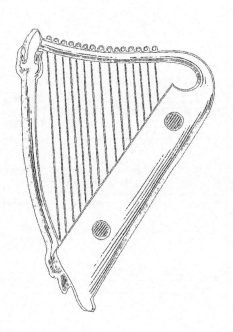

Quant je voi yver

Early 13th C. French

Quant je voi yver

Colin Muset, early 13th C. French carol

Quant je voi yver retourne
lor me voudroi e sejorner,
se je pooie oste trover
large qui ne vousist conter,
qu'e ust porc et buef et mouton,
mas larz faisanz et venoison,
grasses gelines et chapons
et bons fromages en glaon.

When winter comes, so cold and gray,
then I must find a place to stay.
I'll gladly obey a lord who will pay
and give me meals both night and day,
whose dinners are pork and beef and lamb,
duck, pheasant, and deer with marjoram,
fat hens and capons and fine ham,
And cheese in baskets…then glad I am.

Quant voi la flor nouvelle

13th C. France

Quant voi la flor nouvelle

Quant voi la flor nouvele

Anonymous
Pastourelle

Quant voi la flor nouvele
paroir en la praele
et j'oi la fontenele
bruire seur la gravele,
lors mi tient amours nouvele
dont ja ne garai.
Se cist maus ne m'asoage
bien sai qu'en morai.

"Je sui sade et brunette
et jone pucelete;
S'ai coleur vermeillete,
euz verz, bele bouchete;
Si me point la mamelete
que n'i puis durer.
Reson est que m'entremete
des douz maus d'amer.

"Certes, se je trouvoie
qui m'en meist en voie,
volentiers amerois;
Ja por nul nel leroie.
Car bien ai oï retrere,
et por voir conter,
que nus n'a parfete joie
s'el ne vient d'amer."

Vers la tose m'avance
por oïr s'acointance:
Je la vi bele et blanche,
de sinple contenance.
Ne mist pas en oubliance
ce que je li dis.
Maintenant, sanz demorance,
s'amor li requis.

Pris la par la main nue,
mis la seur l'erbe dure;
Ele s'escrie et jure
que de mon gieu n'a cure:
"Ostéz vostre lecheüre!
Dex la puist honir!
Car tant est asprete et dure
ne la puis souffrir."

When I see the new flowers appear in the meadow
and hear the spring rushing on the pebbles,
a new love grips me of which I can never be cured.
If this pain does not recede I know well that I will die of it.

"I am a pleasing and brown-haired young girl.
I have a rosy color, green eyes, a pretty mouthy;
My breast pricks me so that I cannot endure it.
It is right that I should take on the sweet pains of love.

"Indeed, if I were to find someone who could set me on that road,
I would love him willingly; I would never leave him for anyone.
For, indeed, I have heard it said, and claimed as a truth,
that nobody has perfect joy unless it comes from love."

I advanced toward the lass to hear her invitation;
I saw that she was fair and white, with an innocent face.
She did not ignore what I said to her.
At once, without delay, I asked her for her love.

I took her by her bare hand and laid her on the hard grass.
She cried aloud and swore that she cared nothing for my game.
"Stop your wantonness! God make you ashamed of it!
For it is so harsh and hard that I cannot endure it."

Cantiga 82

Alfonso el Sabio X
13th Century Spain

Cantiga 82

Cantiga 82

Como Santa Maria guardou un monge dos diaboos que o quiseran tentar e se lle
mostraron en figures de porcos polo fazer perder.

A Santa Maria mui bon servir faz,
pois o poder ela do demo desfaz.

Ond'av?o desto que en Conturbel
fez Santa Maria miragre mui bel
por un monge bõo, cast' e mui fiel,
que viu de diabres v?ir mui grand' az.
A Santa Maria mui bon servir faz...

En seu leito, u jazia por dormer,
viu-os come porcos contra si v?ir
atan espantosos, que per ren guarir
non cuidava, e dizia-lles: "Az, az,"
A Santa Maria mui servir faz...

El assi estando en mui gran pavor,
viu entrar un ome negro de coor
que diss' aos porcos: "Log' a derredor
dele vos meted', e non dórmia en paz."
A Santa Maria mui bon servir faz...

Eles responderon: "Aquesto fazer
queremos de grado, mais niun poder
de faze-lle mal non podemos aver
por gran santidade que en ele jaz."
A Santa Maria mui servir faz...

E aquel diabo lles respos assi:
"Pois vos non podedes, ar leixad' a mi,
que con estes garfios que eu trag'aqui
o desfarei, pero que trage frocaz."
A Santa Maria mui servir faz...
O frad', est' oyndo, espantou-se mal
e chamou a Virgen, a que nunca fal
aas grandes coitas, dizendo-lle:
"Val me, ca de gran medo ei end'eu assaz."
A Santa Maria mui servir faz...

E a Groriosa tan toste chegou
e ant' aqeul frade logo se parou
e con h?a vara mal am?açou
aquela companna do demo malvaz,
A Santa Maria mui servir faz...

Dizendo: "Come vos ousastes parar
ant' este meu frade neno espantar?
Poren no ynferno ide log' entrar
con vosso mal rey, mui peor que rapaz."
A Santa Maria mui servir faz...

Quant' eles oyron aquesta razon,
como fumo se desfezeron enton;
e a Virgen santa mans' e en bon son
confortou o frade, dizend': "A mi praz
A Santa Maria mui servir faz...

A vida que fazes; e porende ben
faz d'oj' adeante que non leixes ren
de fazeres quant' a ta orden conven."
Esto ditto, tolleu –xe-lle d' ant' a ffaz.
A Santa Maria mui servir faz...

How Holy Mary saved a monk from the devils who tried to tempt him and appeared to him in the form of pigs to make him lose his soul.

It is good to serve Holy Mary, for She destroys the devil's power.
Concerning this, it happened that in Canterbury Holy Mary performed a very beautiful miracle for a good monk, chaste and pious, who saw a great rank of devils approaching.
As he lay in his bed to sleep, he saw them in the form of pigs coming toward him, so frightful that he thought nothing could save him. He said to them: "Get back, get back!"
As he lay there in great terror, he saw a black man enter who said to the pigs: "Place yourselves all around him, do not let him sleep in peace."
They responded: "We will gladly do this, but we can have no power to harm him because of his great saintliness."
That devil replied to them thus: "Well, if you cannot, let me. With these pitchforks that I carry here I shall tear him to bits, even though he wears a silly frock."
The friar, hearing this, became greatly alarmed and called on the Virgin, who never fails in great straits, saying to Her: "Help me, for I am terrified of them!"
The Glorious One arrived at once and stood before that friar and threatened that evil devil's gang with a stick. Saying: "how dare you stand before this friar or frighten him? Go back to Hell with your wicked king who is worse than a thief."
When they heard this order, they vanished like smoke, and the Holy Virgin gently and sweetly comforted the friar, saying: "I am pleased by the life you lead."

Cantiga 100

Alfonso el Sabio X
13th Century Spain

Cantiga 100

49

Cantiga 100
Esta é de loor.

Santa Maria, Strela do dia, mostra-nos via pera Deus e nos guia.

Car veer faze-los errados que perder foran per pecados
entender de que mui culpados son; mais per ti son perdõados
      da ousadia que lles fazia' fazer folia mais que non deveria.

Santa Maria...

Amostrar-nos deves carreira por gãar en toda maneira
a sen par luz e verdadeira que tu dar-nos podes senlleira;
      ca Deus a ti a outorgaria e a querria por ti dar e daria.

Santa Maria...

Guiar ben nos pod' o teu siso mais ca ren pera Parayso
u Deus ten senpre goy' e riso pora quen en el creer quiso;
      e prazaer-m-ia se te prazia que foss' a mia alm'en tal compannia.

Santa Maria...

This is a song of praise.

Holy Mary, Star of Day, show us the way to God and be our guide.

You make the wayward, who were lost because of sin, see and understand that they are very guilty. But they are pardoned by you for the temerity which caused them recklessly to do what they should not.

You must show us the way in all our deeds to win the true and matchless light which only you can give us, for God would grant it to you, and most willingly bestow it for your sake.

Your wisdom can guide us far better than any other thing to Paradise, where God has always delight and joy for whoever would believe in Him. I should rejoice if it please you to let my soul be in such company.

Bailemos

13th Century Portugal

Bailemos

Bailemos
13th C. Portuguese

Bailemos nos ja todas, tres, ai amigas,
so aquestas avelandeiras frolidas,
e quen for velida como nos velidas,
se amigo amar,
so aquestas avelandeiras folidas
verrá bailar.

Bailemos nos ja todas, tres, ai irmanas,
so aqueste ramo destas avelanas,
e quen for louçana como nos louçanas,
se amigo amar,
so aqueste ramo destas avelana
verrá bailar.

Por Deus, ai amigas, mentr'al non fazemos,
so aqueste ramo folido bailemos,
e quen ben parecer como nos parecemos,
se amigo amar,
so aqueste ramo so que nos bailemos
verrá bailar.

Girls, let's dance now, all three of us,
under these blossoming hazel trees,
and any girl who is pretty, as we are,
and who loves a boy,
will come join in the dance
under these blossoming hazel trees.

Sisters, let's dance now, all three of us,
under these spreading hazel branches,
and any girl who is lovely, as we are,
and who loves a boy,
will come join the dance
under these spreading hazel branches.

Girls, for God's sake, let us not delay,
let's dance under these flowering boughs,
and any girl who is fair, as we are
and who loves a boy,
will come join the cane,
under these boughs, where we dance.

Deich von der Guoten Schiet

Friedrich von Hausen

Deich von der Guoten Schiet

Friedrich von Hausen (c. 1155-1190)

Deich von der guoten schiet
Und ich zir niht ensprach
Alsô mir wære liep,
Des lîde ich ungemach.
Daz liez ich durch die diet
Von der mir nît geschah.
Ich wünche ir anders niet,
Wan der die helle brach,
Der füege ir wê und ach.

"Si wænent hüten mîn,
Die sîn doch niht bestât,
Und tuont ir nîden schîn;
Daz wênic si vervât.
Si möhten ê den Rên
Gekêren in den Pfât,
Ê ich mich iemer sîn
Getrôste, swiez ergât,
Der mir gedienet hât."

When I separated from the good woman
and did not speak to her
as I should like to,
that caused me discomfort.
I refrained because of the guardians
from whom I never experienced
anything kind.
Unless he who harrowed hell
would cause them pain and misfortune.

"They think to guard me,
Though it is not their concern,
and show their envy;
that avails them not.
They are more likely
To lead the Rhine
into the Po
before I ever forget the man
Who has served me, come what may."

Meienzit Ane Nit

Neidhart von Reuental

Meienzit Ane Nit

Meienzit Ane Nit

Meienzit Ane Nit

Neidhart von Reuental (1190-1253)

Meienzit ane nit vrouden git wider strit,
sin widerkomen kan uns allen helfen.
uf dem plan ane wan siht man stan wolgetan
liehtiu bruniu bluemel bi den glfen.
durch daz gras sint si schon uf gedrungen,
und der walt manecvalt ungezalt ist erschalt,
daz er wart mit dem nie baz gesungen.

May-time gives joy without hardship;
it's return can help all of us.
In the meadows, indeed,
we see brown-shining flowers beside yellow ones.
They have pieced through the grass,
and the forest repeatedly resounds from
a myriad of voices, as was never before heard.

Ich sung nit nach ir sit, haete ich vrid des ich bit,
ob mir ieman koeme dran ze troste.
ich bin verzeit, miniu leit unverjeit sint so breit;
ich naeme ez noch, swer mich da von erloste,
liebes blic der kan mich schicken wilde.
ez ist min klage alle tage, und gedage als ein zage.
liebes blic, laz mich bi blickes bilde!

I would not have to sing like the birds
if I had the peace that I long for
if only someone would comfort me.
I am disheartened.
My grief is still present and is great.
It would be good if someone rescued me from this grief.
A glace from my beloved can chase me away.
All the time I must complain, but I keep silent like a coward.
Oh, the sight of my love, could I but dwell in her sight!

Ich was vert nach gewert, do ein swert im verrert
ein halbez knie von eim der zen genozen:
enzeman leif in an; kume entran er von dan.
er hat niemer mer kein meit gestozen.
wurde ich noch ze Riuwental gerochen, ich haet heil,
vrouden teil, und waer geil,
ob ein seil im alliu vieriu haete ab gebrochen.

Last year my desire was almost fulfilled
when the sword of one of the ten fellows
cut off half of his kenn. Enzemann attacked him.
He barely escaped,
else he would never again have knocked a girl.
If only I would be avenged in Reuental!
I would be happy and rejoice
when a rope had pulled off all four of his members.

So Blozen wir den Anger

Neidhart von Reuental

So Blozen wir den Anger

So Blozen wir den Anger

Neidhart von Reuental

So blozen wir den anger ligen sahen,
end uns diu liebe zit begunde nahen,
daz die bluomen drungen durch den kle aber als e.
heide diust mit rosen nu bevangen:
den tout der summer wol, niht we.

Droschel, nahtigal die hoert man singen,
von ir schalle berc unt tal erklingen:
si vreunt sich gegen der lieben sumerzit,
diu uns git vreuden vil und liehter ougenweide,
diu heide wunneclichen lit.

Sprach ein maget: "die wissen wellent touwen,
megt ir an dem summer wunder schouwen?
die boume, die den winder stounden val,
uber al sint si niuwes loubes worden riche:
dar under singent nahtigal.

Losa, wie die vogele alle doenent,
wie si den meien mit ir sange kroenent!
Ja, waen ich, der winder ende hat.
Wierat, sprine also, daz ich dir simmer danke!
diu linde wol geloubet stat.

Da sul wir uns wider hiuwer zweien.
vor dem walde ist rosen vil geheien:
der wil ich ein kranzel wolgetan ufe han,
springe ich einem ritter an der hende in hohem muote.
nu wol dran!"

"Tohterlin, la dich sin niht gelangen!
wil du die ritter an dem reien drangen,
die dir niht ze maze ensulen sin, tohterlin,
du wirst an dem schaden wol ervunden.
der junge meier muotet din."

"Sliezet mir den meier an die versen!
ja truwe ich stolzem ritter wol gehersen:
zwiu sol ein gebuwer mir ze man?
der enkan mich nach minem willen niht getriuten:
er, waen, min eine muoz gestan."

"Tohterlin, la dir in niht versmalen!
du wilt ze tumbe ritters kunde vahen:
daz ist allen dinen vriunden leit.
manegen eit swuere du: des wis nu ane lougen,
din muot dich allez von mir treit!"

"Muoter min, ir lazet iuwer bagen!
ich wil mine vriunde durch in wagen,
den ich minen willen nie verhal.
uber al muezen sin die liute warden inne:
min muot der strebt gein Riuwental."

Bare was the meadow when we looked at it
until that lovely time approached when
the flowers pierced through the clover, as ever.
Now the heath is lined with roses:
the summer does them good, not harm.

One can hear thrushes and nightingales sing;
from their song mountains and valleys resound:
They rejoice over the lovely summertime,
which gives us much happiness and feasts our eyes.
Wonderfully lies the heath.

Said a maiden: "The meadows will thaw.
Can you see the marvels of summer?
The trees, bare during the winter,
are now abundant with new leaves
and the nightingales sing in their branches.

Listen, how the birds burst into song,
crowning May with their voices;
Yes, I believe winter has come to an end.
Maiden Wierat, spring and dance so that I may
always thank you for it!
The linden stands there full of leaves.

There we should come together again.
In front of the forest many roses have grown.
From them I will wear a well-made little chaplet
when dancing with pride at the hand of a knight.
Well then!"

"Young daughter, do not long for a knight.
Will you throng among knights in the round-dance?
They are not for you, young daughter,
for you will soon suffer harm.
The young Meier wants you."

"Take the young Meier out of my way!
I can well have a proud young knight for company:
How could I get along with a peasant as a husband?
He could not caress me as I would like;
He will have to be without me!"

Young daughter, do not distain him!
How stupid to want a knight!
All your friends are sorry about that.
You have often sworn not to do it.
 Keep to your promise now!
Otherwise your wantonness will take you from me!"

"Stop your scolding, mother,
for him I will put my friends to the test.
I have never concealed my intention to them.
Everywhere people shall know:
My being tends towards Reuental."

Ballo Francese

Giorgio Mainerio 1578

Ballo Francese

Pour quoy

Ronde

T. Susato

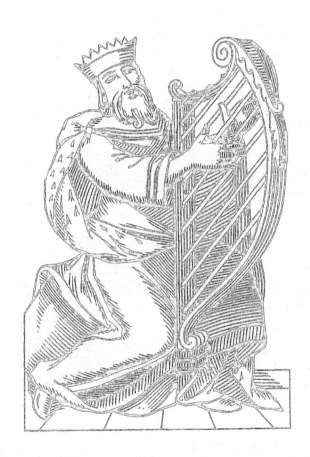

Putta Nera

Ballo Furlano

Giorgio Mainerio 1578

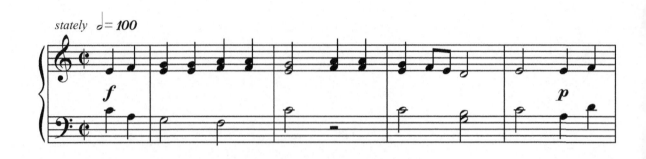

Putta Nera

Speme Amorosa

G.G. Gastoldi 1596

Si pas souffrir

Pavan

Harp

Ronde # 4

T. Susato

About the Author

Laura Zaerr teaches both pedal harp and folk harp at the University of Oregon, where she obtained her bachelor's degree in music performance and composition. She holds a master's degree in harp performance from the Eastman School of Music, where she studied with Eileen Malone.

Over the past 20 years Laura has produced several solo CDs featuring original compositions and arrangements of Celtic tunes. She has also recorded collaboratively with various musical groups including the Oregon Renaissance Band, and Trilogy, a Celtic band.

As well as maintaining a thriving studio in Oregon, Laura travels throughout the Northwest giving workshops and concerts. In her spare time she enjoys white-water kayaking.

photo by Bob Furguson

Printed in Great Britain
by Amazon

33518369R00051